LIBERTY

poems by

C. Prudence Arceneaux

Finishing Line Press
Georgetown, Kentucky

LIBERTY

Copyright © 2021 by C. Prudence Arceneaux
ISBN 978-1-64662-522-2 First Edition
All rights reserved under International and Pan-American Copyright Conventions. No part of this book may be reproduced in any manner whatsoever without written permission from the publisher, except in the case of brief quotations embodied in critical articles and reviews.

ACKNOWLEDGMENTS

I am grateful to *The Texas Observer* for publishing "My Cousin Dies Like a Deer, On the Side of the Road."

Publisher: Leah Huete de Maines
Editor: Christen Kincaid
Cover Art: Anastasia Patience Hobbs
Author Photo: Mark A. Ansualda
Cover Design: Michael Chang

Order online: www.finishinglinepress.com
also available on amazon.com

Author inquiries and mail orders:
Finishing Line Press
PO Box 1626
Georgetown, Kentucky 40324
USA

Table of Contents

Nasa Needs Poets 1

When Someone Decides Your Black Life Doesn't Matter 2

My Cousin Dies, Like a Deer, On the Side of the Road 4

When Asked How I Feel Now That I'm On Lexapro 5

Dust Void 7

Picking Corn 10

How to Be Politically Correcteed 13

Liberty 14

"The Cause of the Fire is Under Investigation" 15

liberty 1 the quality or state of being free a: the power to do as one pleases b: freedom from physical restraint c: freedom from arbitrary and despotic control d: the positive enjoyment of various social, political or economic rights e: the power of choice

NASA Needs Poets

What I wouldn't give for the chance to sail the void—
I'd let myself get yawed, learn more languages (I am

already fluent in English and Grief.), learn how
to vomit in a bag, to shield myself from too much light.

I've trained my whole life to live in confined space.
But I'll settle for being the first to talk up the musky

promises of terran land under Grand Canyon- red Martian
skies, debate on CNN which atmosphere is most toxic: Venus

or Earth. Oh, to be a meteorologist of Jupiter! Surely, even
I can be right 30% of the time.

I'll start every poem with the image of the star- eating
black hole, burping four million tons of life stuff, silently

shouting heartbeats and future tense. Truly, I was born
with an understanding of the subtleties of darkness,

and a need to know: Can you see hate from space?
I want to proclaim the truth of dark matter. Yes, your lord said,

"Let there be light," but there is so much more that is dark,
terrifyingly simple, not knowing what is true North other

than what we've said, of "We have been wrong." "Again."
To be the harbinger of our savage hunger when we make it

to Europa and taint its amniotic seas, extoll the paths of dark
energy that weave through the light, making highways, making

signposts, we should follow! Does it matter what Pluto is
if we don't know what we are? Makemake whispers revelations

in my ears! You'll see—they'll want me on the payroll
as we expand into the never ending never ending never ending never

When Someone Decides Your Black Life Doesn't Matter

You wake to the news of another man murdered.
The reports say there are two contagions we battle;
is it simple contagion if it's been in the blood so long?

It's been pandemic for centuries;
we need a new word.
You try to shuck the fear of plague you carry,

every human you pass adds a small thing—a pea here,
a root there, melon- heavy, and only your people seem
able to find its ripeness. You watch as skins are slopped,

for hogs, composted before it became gentrified, before
anyone asked how this soil became so fertile.
Home is colored glass, assumption, but the weight

of each person's singularity shatters its light.
The mosquito bites get to you, the small injections of hate
—how your skin quivers when you slap it, beat it,

cover it with your own blood—the numbness overrides.
And the welts of years rise on your flesh, swollen,
throbbing. What did your grandmother say would soothe this itch?

Your mother asks which town has the sign that reminds
niggers to be gone by dark. (Your hubris says because
you are not a nigger, you could stay overnight.) You list

Jasper
Kountze
Vidor

Silsbee
Pine Forest
She interrupts, in a voice that ghost-echoes, you are wrong

wrong wrong; you remind her specificity doesn't matter.
Schools don't teach which tools are better to pierce
the skin—knife, rod, adze. Or which tool best

removes head from body—rope, chain, ax. As if
you were vampires. Submerge the bodies in the holy
river waters of The Trinity.   Do we rise?
                    Do you sink?

You know this is a poem for your impending death,
a poem for those who prepared the way for you.
This poem is an anagram.

Let them find the names.

My Cousin Dies, Like a Deer, On the Side of the Road

"The Texas Department of Public Safety (DPS) is asking for help from the public in the investigation of a fatal hit-and-run crash that resulted in the death of a pedestrian on FM 160 east of FM 2830. The crash occurred at approximately 11:00 p.m., Sunday June 14." Bluebonnet News

You must have been a thing of beauty:
among the hoots, clicks, whistles of swamp-
land dark, then spotlighted, machina-
flung, crescent body, eclipsing, rising—
nyxnaut—occluding white pores in velvet
night nap. Such silence   all listening
to the luminous staccato, 270 bones, rapturous
vibrato, soul—too long in marrow—released.

No one knows when to applaud.
                        Then:

                                          chirrup

When Asked How I Feel Now That I'm On Lexapro

1
Imagine a line—horizontal.
It goes from there to here.
Then bisect it with another line
—vertical. I let you pick the angles.
Bear with me, please;
we are graphing a life:
nounly, verbly, reflexively, participly.
I now care 35.53% less than I did.
I already cared 63.82% less than other people.
I'm just our side of dead.

I gloam about, clouds like Stevie Nicks scarves
waving from my arms. Days are newspaper grey.
I avoid the color inserts; they all burst red: candy
apple, cerise, tomato, amaranth, cinnabar, fire
brick, vermillion, lava, tomato, lipstick, fire engine.
Can't even look at the comics anymore.

2
You should work at the grief in you, like pick to hurt tooth,
digging metal in again and again, seek the meat, the pulp.
And pace yourself.

The first thrust against the rot will walk
breath from your mouth. You'll stop. Don't
wipe the tears when you start again. This is a fluid business.

If you were in your person clothes, you would note
the absurdity of this choice, but you are in your skin
clothes; don't think much, overly long.

Do what a doctor would do.
Dig in again, seek the edge of the root,
are you too afraid to commit?

Practice sounds you make—
groan, whimper, shriek, moan, scream.
It is unseemly to make a show of yourself.

Remember: you are not a doctor.
There is no doctor to cure this.

Dust Void

three pairs of underwear
five pairs of socks
can opener
Other states don't want Texans.
Other countries don't want Americans.
Who wants black people?
ultrathin jacket
crank radio
work gloves
passport
Your mother moved in last May. You've been packed for years.
You don't tell her, didn't want her mouse- like. She sleep-
screams when fear vacations with her.
two toothbrushes
first aid kit
water bottle
pepper spray
You bought rain ponchos the day after they murdered Breonna Taylor.
deck of cards
map of texas
meds
wax pencil
The persistent season in your gut belches warnings this will happen
at night. You don't close your eyes until the sky is watercolored
some lighter shade of awareness.
a comb
granola bars
toothpaste (make that two)
matches
The law says throw away a driver license when it expires.
You have four. Put one in your bra, one on your sole
in your sock, one in your underwear. In case someone
tries to remove who you are.
rice

water purification tablets
two pairs of jeans
ammo
You want to ask her to pack. The rusted rigor of your sleep is soundtracked with wet belts on her soft neck, the knock of her temple on concrete, the repeated gurgle of her throat blocked by her own breath.
space blanket
hat
book of edible plants
knife
When Dad died, she cleansed the house of him. Seed and hammer, suits and shoes, ashtrays and beer cans. You kept his pocket knife.
pack of condoms
gun
rubber bands
jerky
She'll sugar- ant when it happens, suddenly concerned with the provenance of a shoe horn, rubber ducky, glass pitcher, plastic hanger. It won't be the last time you wonder how you'll live or how you'll both die.
four gold coins
watch
tea
magnet
You are prepared to barter with your body.
two black t- shirts
beans
flashlight
rope
mirror
She doesn't sense the way the air pants. You ask her

to strengthen arms, legs. 75 years of knowledge, heavy
in her bosom. At least her cane can be a weapon.
glow sticks
oatmeal
sun screen
glasses
You know you will forget your glasses. You can't see,
you won't look. It will be your history. If anyone hears it.
That you couldn't see your salvation right in front of you.
salt
lighter
compass
black sweatshirt
soap
Humans can live for a week without food.
Humans can live for three days without water.
How long can a human sustain on fear?

Picking Corn

I
In the middle of my lecture I find
myself warning students away from
corn fields. All fields, really, but my
warning breeds from my grandfather's
fields: the high, thin stalks, like legs
on starved bodies, scuttle of husky
dried skin, the freckles you carry
home.

It's the last part, the least poetic, that
makes me stop, not because I am so
caught in my flesh- dreams of hoeing
burrows, half circles of blood under
nails, but the entire class is watching
me, the ovals of their faces reflecting
waxy into my eyes, blotted features.
Some are tilted to the side. The only
things missing
                              —cocked
ears, furrowed brows.

II
This isn't the semester, pacing the field between podium and desk,
I have to announce, "You know, I'm not a slave!"

This isn't the semester I have to explain "ultimate grandmother."

This isn't the semester I have to define Creole from Cajun.

This is the semester the ovals squint every time I claim "black."

I understand the ovoid confusion, when copper strands in my hair
stand coarse and spiked like nettles, when skin flakes at the battle
line between what is French in me, what is Indian—an old fight still.
I don't think they even hear the question scurrying under their words:
"How black are you?"

I'm not good at math.
                              Enough.

III
I'm still talking about Jefferson's words,
the great experiment he envisioned, slowed
my speech, careful to cut my T's, breathe
through my nose between words. Though I am
East Texas in my saliva, in my teeth, in my tongue,
it shouldn't have taken them so long to realize
I said, "I don't have time for chiggers."

How to Be Politically Corrected

Jemima lost her job. No union to negotiate,
to advocate, for her. (No one could afford her dues.)

The last time they tried to let her go, they told her
she needed a new look. So she melted her hair, made

it flat, no scarf to keep off the heat from their kitchens,
protect her soon- frizzy hair ("Inappropriate Work Hairstyles"

—someone googled it for her.) She bought fake pearls, some oily
brown now from the make-up she learned she should wear.

They told her she had to change her clothes if she was gonna
come into their homes; she did, wearing her good clothes, soaking

up the smells of their houses: cat piss, patchouli, baby vomit, her own
sweat yellowing the back of her collar. More than ever she thought

burn it all before she walked over her own porch.
The job wasn't great, the job wasn't good, but she kept showing up

for breakfast whenever they needed her: the 630am bus driver, the 3am
shift work disorder, the 730am "You need a good breakfast; testing

this week!" Now days, not in the cloying sweetness of early
morning memories, work that moved her from rent to food to doctor,

but on hold, proceeding online, writing letters, repeating 7- 4- 8,
learning how to spell her new last name U- N- E- M- P- L- O- Y- E- D,

and trying not to look too closely at the front page of the paper to see
what sunny face will replace hers.

The Nadinola coupon falls to the floor.

Liberty

Exxon comes calling. *It's a simple thing,*
the woman says, her voice soft, like her name—
Lash—*a small corner of land*, they want,
No rights, they swear, *but can't have it back,*

and we all have to agree— living aunt, living
uncle, and cousins, who mix like peppers and oil,
like chicken legs in gumbo. This woman
knows things we don't know. Have our ancestors'

bodies decayed like dinosaurs, under land-bound
oppression: hand, lungs, heart, blood: an oil
held in the earth? She wants us to sell off blood-
deeds. How do you put on the market the soil

that makes up your scarf skin?:
      "The wet wool sky will always keep you sheltered,
      the water makes you fertile. The previous owners
      lost two young, the others thrived. That elm punched
      up through the family room space for growth,
      an ever- present almanac. Wasps—flying blood
      drops—are your home security. Fire ant mounds,
      sentinels, ever vigilant. You learn, to your left,
      always, those are bones, those are roots;
      careful how your children play."

This woman is as needed as a buzzard, circling the rot
in our soil. Her commission will come from the ma
between our skins and our souls. She knows it,

and her voice is hard, like her last name—Lash. Exxon
knows the freedom she offers, whittling fancy
our slip- grip hold on the deed. A tear- like dribble
of ink, we could rid ourselves of land, of family, of history.

"The Cause of the Fire is Under Investigation."
    –NPR

Strike

    against buildings.
    against boots.
    against streets.

Watch what happens in your hands.

It will not go out
   without burning you.

C. Prudence Arceneaux, a native Texan, is a poet who has taught at Austin Community College, in Austin, TX, since 1998. She earned a BA in English/ Creative Writing from the University of New Mexico, but even before finishing the degree realized "there's no place like home." Upon her return to Texas, she began work on an MFA in Creative Writing, which she received from the University- formerly- known- as- Southwest- Texas- State in 1998. Her work has appeared in various journals, including *Limestone, New Texas, Clark Street Review, Hazmat Review* and *Inkwell*. Her chapbook *DIRT* was award the 2018 Jean Pedrick Prize.

www.ingramcontent.com/pod-product-compliance
Lightning Source LLC
LaVergne TN
LVHW041526070426
835507LV00013B/1845